HOME SCHOOL ME

Home School Me

Homeschool Guide: A Choice for Parents, Offering Support Through Experience

Kimberly Mathurin

Kimberly Mathurin
Book Designer
Rooted Learning Books

Contents

Preface

Thinking of homeschooling or currently homeschooling?

This book is designed to be an informative and helpful guide to begin or continue your journey in elective home education (EHE). It will help you build confidence, generate ideas and give you a push if you are currently homeschooling. It's a useful book to help you stay motivated and assist you in the process. This book can also help you gain an insight into what homeschooling has to offer; highlighting the benefits but also discussing the struggles that can come along the way. It can help you to evaluate your processes and create new ideas for your home learning study programme in the US, U.K., and perhaps worldwide.

As a home educator in the U.K, I use my career skills to promote a healthy learning environment. I have a background in teaching for over ten years, with a focus on adult learning from basic literacy pre-entry to level 2 in both maths and English. I then went on to teach a range of subjects such as health and social care, employability skills and I.T. You do not need these skills to homeschool your child; all you need is a passion for your child's education; a few resources, and a safe and comfortable learning environment at home.

My passion for teaching comes from my natural ability to be able to explain things to people in a way that allows them to gain a good understanding of the message I was trying to convey. I understood that things had to be explained in different ways for different people, as we all have different learning styles, but we also can have different learning needs. I felt that I would be able to help somebody understand my topic or piece of information with more certainty than ever before if it was something that I was knowledgeable about. Being able to pass that information on, and the learner "gets it," prompted my journey into adult literacy. I began training adults through my local council in adult learning centres, and working with people who found it difficult to read and write. I began teaching as a support tutor until I became qualified and then went on to teach at various learning institutions, in different subjects that I was educated in.

Alongside this career, I was also a career consultant, which allowed me to work personally with an individual. Meeting people from a range of backgrounds, educational and career levels, enhanced my knowledge of the education system and structure. Having to be knowledgeable in many areas, such as career markets, interviewing techniques, CV writing, and educational routes were part of my skillset. I then went on to specialise in assistive technology, which is aimed at university students who may struggle with physical or mental health, have learning difficulties, are neurodiverse etc. I'm currently on a journey to becoming an educational psychologist.

In reflection, my career choices would suggest that I am a person who likes to help others progress. This may also be the reason I have taken the time out to perfect and write this book but I also feel the need to help others in this journey that I embarked on, once my son left nursery age.

I decided to homeschool for two main reasons. My son did not enjoy the nursery experience and I had a period in my life when I was homeschooled. My son never wanted to go to nursery, he would always be upset when I dropped him off. He would throw a tantrum or cry. I did not enjoy leaving him but I did enjoy the freedom I felt once I had dropped him off, knowing it would be a few hours until I picked him up. My mother told me that I cried every time she dropped me to nursery but now being the mother and no longer the child, the tables had turned and I felt guilty at times, but I assumed he was in safe hands. However, the upset never stopped and continued for the two

years he attended. Interestingly, the nursery assistants informed me that he was well-behaved and seemed fine throughout the day. I started to consider homeschooling as an option once the nursery informed me of the timing of the application process for my son to begin school. I was leaning towards homeschooling, as it felt that he was perhaps not ready to begin the school journey in an institution which he might find daunting.

As a child, I went through three different types of schooling: public school, private school and homeschool. My homeschool experience was for a short period in my childhood, so I was not new to the idea, and my sister had already taken the decision to homeschool her children. Therefore, for me, it was natural to give it a try and also for me to give my son a positive experience of learning after being so miserable at nursery. Attending public school, private school, homeschooling, and then back into public school was a bit daunting in the end. I remember my year 4 public school teacher telling my mum, 'Sorry we just don't do work at this level,' after she had shown her some of my maths worksheets that were aimed at GCSE standards, having attended a private school.

I remember having to let go of knowledge I already knew in order to blend into the class, which didn't take long as a child, because I simply didn't care. The key takeaway from this is that, when education is less regimented, our ability can take us further.

It is an amazing feeling when you teach your child to read, and it can be very motivating at that early stage as you are devoted to the education progress of your child from the beginning. You are constantly nurturing their interests and teaching topics in a way that is right for you and your child, and as a result, watching them become smarter and grow in confidence. As a parent, it can feel amazing as you learn your child's strengths and weaknesses. Hopefully, this book will give you the confidence to believe in your ability to educate your child, too.

P.S. There are learning strategies and support tools mentioned throughout, to assist you on your journey. Most resources mentioned in this book can be found in the last

chapter (chapter 13: Useful Resources)

Chapter 1

Getting Started

Congratulations on your choice to homeschool! (otherwise known as home educate). After all, homeschooling is a fantastic option for parents who want to take the lead or be actively involved in their child's learning and development. This choice may stem from personal preference or arise as a default option based on individual circumstances. It's always crucial to check with your local government and the rules governing homeschooling before you begin.

In the U.K., if your child does not start formal school education, then legally (in 2024), you do not need to inform your local authority of your decision to homeschool. However, you can do so voluntarily if you choose. If your child is already in school and you wish to homeschool, you are not required to inform the school about your decision, but it would be in your best interest to do so. The school is obligated to notify your local authority of the reason for your child's removal. This procedure helps address any concerns regarding how your child will continue their education. Understanding these regulations ensures that you can proceed with confidence, allowing you to focus on creating a supportive and enriching learning environment tailored to your child's needs.

My aim with this book is to alleviate any overwhelming feelings or stress associated with the concept of homeschooling, as well as to share my homeschooling experience, and offer advice to assist in finding one's own path when educating at home. There are ignorant views that a school (institution) environment is the only place a child can learn. This is not true. The world provides a rich learning environment, and apart from curriculum-based learning, life itself is our greatest teacher through play, interaction with others, and travel. The list goes on, and there's absolutely no need to feel guilty or adopt others' opinions on what you feel is best for your child.

You may be surprised to know that some schools allow children to attend on a different schedule or part-time basis, which can help ease the transition into homeschooling. Perhaps your child has a learning difficulty or health condition, leading you to feel that they are not receiving the right support. This could encourage you to explore alternative options that better suit their individual needs. Ultimately, embracing homeschooling can open doors to tailored learning experiences that prioritise your child's well-being and interests, allowing them to thrive in a nurturing environment designed just for them.

An 'Autodidact' is someone who learns on their own. Your child/children may have a natural thirst for knowledge that stems from outside of formal institutions, allowing you to tailor your child's learning to their interests and requirements based on you and your child's lifestyle. One of the main concerns presented by parents hoping to homeschool is that they work and do not have the opportunity to homeschool so they can't.

This is a myth. Of course, money is needed to run a house, keep a house and homeschool, however, if you can present yourself with the barriers you face, you also have the power to eliminate the barriers you face; you first need to be sure of your decision and plan for it if you are already caught up in the system. See the possibilities around you. There are now more opportunities to work from home than ever before.

If you have family support, then make use of it, or even network with other like-minded parents. They can be found online through social media or on neighbour apps such as Nextdoor. It is true, changes will need to be made but can also be seen as adaptations to suit your lifestyle. I'm sure everyone's homeschool situation is unique and doesn't follow any set pattern or order. A good suggestion is to ask your workplace if your role could be moved to working from home or a part home/ part work schedule as you are considering homeschooling your child. You may be surprised to see things work out for you once you've set the intention. Just remember, if others are doing it, then it can be done.

Have I Made The Right Choice

You may be wondering if you have made the right choice deciding to homeschool. The question to answer is if you have decided to homeschool before putting your child into an institution, or are you removing your child from an institution to homeschool? The best way to decide is to write down the pros and cons for both. Your reasons are valid, so if you feel the pros of homeschooling outweigh the cons then it will be a good idea to proceed. You can always put your child into school at a later date.

In the U.K., Section 7 of the 'Education Act' 1996 makes clear that a "child of compulsory school age shall cause him to receive efficient full-time education suitable ... either by regular attendance at school or otherwise".

Compulsory school age is 5 years old. More info regarding the law can be found through the registered charity, 'Child Law Advice', and also with your local authority. There is no legal definition for 'full-time', 'efficient' or 'suitable' education, nor can suitable or efficient education be seen as the same thing.

You are NOT required to:

1. Set hours

2. Prepare a timetable

3. Observe school hours

4. Formally assess progress

Therefore, in order to meet section 7 of the 'Education Act 1996' you must be able to demonstrate a quantifiable amount of time for homeschooling. Remember, one to one contact is around the clock as well as learning opportunities. Suitability should meet the child's age, ability, aptitude and needs in your view, as parents. The U.K. government has introduced a new 'Children's Wellbeing Bill' which local authorities will have to adhere to. This means, keeping a record of home-schooled children such as a register, and providing support to parents. More information can be found on the Gov.uk website. Because it is still a bill and not yet legislation, you must stay informed of when it goes into effect.

For the USA, there has been a huge increase in homeschooling. The NHERI (National Home Education Research Institute) provides statistics and research facts on home education in the USA. It explains that home educated children can score 15-25 percentile points above public schooled students on standardized tests. You must check with your state on the requirements for homeschooling.

It's good for both parents to be involved in the decision making, if possible, as both parents could support the child/children if homeschooling is ideal. We all have strengths in different areas and it is good for a child to get taught by more than one person from time to time, in line with the old saying, 'It takes a village to raise a child'. However, if you are a single parent, it is still possible to homeschool with good time management and educational support services if preferred, which will be presented in a later chapter. Separated parents who may not agree on what schooling option is best should seek mediation services and if all fails then both parents can apply to the courts as part of a child arrangement order.

I've read amazing things about homeschooled children achieving more than children in public schools and surpassing them. I've never heard anything negative about homeschooling, so I didn't have that mindset. However, if you've been given a negative view of homeschooling, have a think of where you heard it from because it could be the reason why you may feel afraid of going ahead or discouraged.

One of the main points I heard from others when I told them that I was homeschooling my child was, "what about their interaction?" Which seems to be people's main concern. Homeschool does not mean keeping your child indoors and away from other children. Now, if you have only one child and homeschool them, they will most likely not have social interaction with other children their age at home during school hours, but they will also not be influenced or impacted by children at school either. Interestingly, people's main concern is not the education, if you have more than one child at home.

Assuming a child at school spends the day interacting with friends and studying, and is content with this arrangement, it may appear that your child is missing out. However, having friends and family whose children are in school and learning alongside their peers, I have seen that the children are not always happy. Hence, it is important to clarify your reasons for homeschooling. It may be a good idea to ask children around you who are of primary school age (whether they are your friends' children or family members) how they feel about school in order to gather some qualitative data.

It is a misapprehension that learning and social interaction with peers must be merged, as they are two independent situations. To elaborate, if your child is learning well at home, it does not imply that your child lacks social interaction or has poor social skills. Thus, if your child is learning in a social setting, it does not necessarily mean that your child is doing well with their learning. A child's social life depends on active parents/carers engaging the child into social aspects of life

Check in on your child's welfare, always! Feelings of isolation for a child can occur in a social setting such as school as it's true that not all children who go to school interact well with others and build relationships. If you are talking in class, you may be given a detention. You are given around one hour and a half to socialise which includes eating lunch. More socialisation can take place before school starts and afterschool. As an adult, you will be advised to have a social life outside of work known as the work life balance. Extracurricular activities and social clubs can aid with social interaction but that also depends on what your child enjoys. Social interaction can also occur in the family home amongst friends of the family and family members such as cousins etc. They may also play within their neighbourhood with local children if there are grounds available where children can play.

There are camps for the holidays and places to learn skills and interact through your local council, or paid for club activities to become involved with. Overall, there will always be good and bad experiences as we are all individuals trying to figure it out. The intention is that you want the best for your child and there's nothing wrong with that.

Resources You May Need To Begin

Decide where schooling will take place within your home, i.e., bedroom, living room, study, or office. Everyone's home is different so it's vital to pick the best or most comfortable part of your home that will provide adequate lighting and fits a desk or table. You may prepare this space over multiple rooms. You may want to get creative. For example, my child's learning environment has a world map poster on the wall, the desk is part of a newly designed book shelf and we have stuck colourful wall art stickers within the area to create a child friendly learning environment. This could be an arts and craft activity for you and your child to enjoy together as part of a project that can give personal satisfaction.

On the desk, my son has access to a pot of pens, pencils, felt pens, colouring pencils, rubber, sharpener, ruler and calendar. We have stuck our learning schedule on the wall which is a planner for our learning times/days which I will discuss further in a later chapter. Each subject would benefit from its own book and you and your child could have fun decorating it as part of arts and craft.

I store away in a small box, things associated with arts and crafts such as; straws, coloured paper, paint, PVA glue, cello tape, tissue paper, etc. Alternatively, you could get a B5 project book, also known as a Pukka Pad, which will separate your different projects or subjects for you within the same pad. Or it could be used for one specific subject, such as science, which can be broken down into different areas like animals, electricity, plants, etc.

Some of these pads also have a planner on the front page which you can fill in with your learning routine for the week. Work books are a good option and are old school but perfect for homeschooling. Depending on your child's age, they also come with stickers such as stars, which are good for placing on each completed page; it also gives your child encouragement and lets them know symbolically that they have done a good job.

It is a good idea to keep a diary in the form of a folder, if preferred. You may use this to track your child's progress monthly, termly, or just whenever you feel like it. I have found this useful as it shows me a journey of progression, my child's weaknesses, areas to focus on, or just an overview of what has been achieved. I include how my child feels about different subjects/topics which allows me to plan things towards his needs, and his interests. I tend to write in the style of a diary because I prefer to flow in the moment and I find it to be a good reflective exercise. Please follow what feels right for you, whether it be formal or informal; the idea is to assist you on your practice and your child's experience.

Please see the list below for the resources mentioned above:

- Pens
- Pencils
- Felt Pens
- Colouring Pencils
- Sharpener
- Ruler

- Calendar

- Rubber

- Small box

- Straws

- Coloured Paper

- Paint

- PVA Glue

- Cello Tape

- Tissue Paper

- B5 Project Book/Pukka Pad

- Workbooks

- Folder

Providing A Learning Environment

One of the cool things about homeschooling a child is that you get to almost become a child again yourself! It is useful to reminisce on your old childhood and school days in order to get a feel, and remember the things you enjoyed when you were learning. What things do you remember on the walls? What colours were inviting? How did you like to sit? What type of activities were fun?

This is how you can create a learning environment for your child that is encouraging and playful. I remember in primary school we all had drawers with our first and last name on laminated paper at the front and that is where we stored our individual classwork or personal items for the day. Perhaps your child can have a special drawer with their name on it so they can store their items, and work. I remember how it made me feel; I felt like I had a special section in the classroom that was mine. I was able to avoid losing things because I had somewhere to put my incomplete work, which made me feel responsible for my work.

A learning environment isn't just about the décor or furniture arrangement. as learning takes place all around us. Learning is wherever you see an opportunity for your child to learn. When you are homeschooling, you will naturally find these opportunities present themselves more and more, such as food shopping at your local grocery store. There are a range of vegetables and fruits to explore as well as the ability to identify vegetable plant families, which is great for the visual learner.

If money management is part of your learning plan, shopping is a great opportunity to allow them to use their money skills, such as paying for an item with their pocket money at the till. Should they have cash and a child debit card in a wallet, they can use their money management skills to decide if they have enough cash to pay, or need to pay by card. Child debit cards can be linked to online apps where they can check their balance ahead of time or alternatively, at cash ATMs.

If they have cash, they can use their problem-solving skills to work out how much change they have left, or by card, they can work out how much money is left on their account if they were aware of the balance before the deduction. I find the store cashiers to be of great assistance when my child pays for something. They are quite impressed, and also very helpful and patient.

This helps your child to grow confident in areas of life that are important to their personal development, and it is also great for the kinaesthetic learner. Sometimes whilst shopping, items in the store may be moved to other areas and it can be difficult trying to find where they are. However, this can be turned into a learning activity for your child, allowing them to ask a nearby store representative where a particular item is. Have them listen to the instructions on where to go and what aisle and then allow your child to lead the way. Great for the auditory learner.

Research

It is a good idea to listen to other people's accounts of homeschooling, and you can easily find some like-minded social groups if you don't know anyone directly whom you could talk to. Perhaps someone you know, knows someone who is currently homeschooling their child or children. It seems that, as time progresses more and more people are considering the idea and may also be looking for other similar minds.

If you are on a few social media sites, it would be good to search for groups or pages that can provide helpful information in your area, and just to have the opportunity to feel supported. A few resources can be found in the resource section of this book. Doing it completely alone could make you wonder if you are doing the right thing but when you break out from social norms then this can become a normal feeling which lets you know that, 'yes' you are doing the right thing for you and your child. Because you decided to, and life has no guarantees, so you have a right to try things out and make decisions that best suit your family. I'm not suggesting to gamble with your child's education; maybe it will work, maybe it will not.

You will have your highs and lows, perhaps more highs than lows if you understand that navigating your way through homeschooling is part of the beauty, as your options are unlimited for what your child can learn and how your child learns. We are very fortunate to have the internet at our finger tips where we can research something new or find out something instantly, that we did not already know. If you feel your homeschooling will benefit with more structure, then add it, if less, then remove some and gain more insight as you go along.

Many families had the experience of homeschooling across the globe during the pandemic, which made the world less ignorant to the idea, and now it is a fact that more people than ever before have a homeschool experience with their child. Some may have even continued to do so, especially if it was something they wanted to do before, and having been forced into it, realised that they were able to achieve this goal on a full-time basis.

There are tutors that can visit your home and educate your child in a specific subject (this may be costly) or learning environments such as 'explore Learning' often found in Sainsbury's or local areas offering tuition in English and maths (this involves a monthly fee by direct debit). There are charities for advice and specialised learning course material providers such as 'Oxford Homeschooling'. Nevertheless, homeschooling also gives you the opportunity to revisit lost information since your schoolyears, and begin the revision process as you teach your child. This can help to keep your mind active in this area once again.

Chapter 2

What Should I Include In The Study Programme?

It would appear that even though your child is not enrolled in school, they still need to study the core curriculum for school. Wrong! This is not compulsory, although you may use it as a guide. This could involve focusing on the subjects the school offers, or at least some of the content you feel is important and useful.

You may decide to use the curriculum as a guide in line with your child's age and what is being taught i.e. maths. Your child does not have to be at that same level, they may be under or above. Maths may not be one of your child's strengths, but would you like your child to have basic maths skills. Yes! It would benefit them in real life situations and also challenge their brain, as maths includes a lot of problem solving and is also a good way for them to understand money (if we still have coins and plastic in our wallets), in this rapidly changing digital world.

There is not a particular route you must take for your study programme. You now have the opportunity to create your own programme. Just like a Saturday school or a private school would. For example, you might follow the core curriculum for maths and English but introduce coding or fine arts, depending on your child's interests or developing skills. A good idea is to first write down in a list what you would like your child to learn at that point in time, considering their age, interests and ability.

This allows learning to be fun for the child but also motivating for the parent to teach and engage. Your teaching style may be more practical, auditorial, or visual depending on your preferred teaching style or your child's learning style, which I will explain further in a later chapter. The different learning styles will allow you to create different types of lessons or activities. For instance, studying Van Gogh (the painter) you may find yourself outside in the community admiring different flowers and if you live nearby in London, visiting the area where he grew up to see the gardens dedicated in his name, as opposed to just searching for information on the internet.

Revision is the key to learning. As an assistive technology tutor, I tell my students that the real learning takes place once they begin practising the software, making their mistakes and rectifying it. Revision is repetitive, as you would have to explore it before hand in order to revise it. It would be an ideal way of learning by including it into your study programme for the week. I guarantee you positive results in practice, similar to the school curriculum; if you study it, you will notice a pattern.

As they progress with age the same materials are repeated but to a higher standard and in greater depth, to match their progress and ability. Don't be disheartened if your child forgets something you taught them two days ago or even last week. This is common amongst children as they are learning things for the first time and also learning to retain that new information. They do not yet have the practical skills of where to place this information, but as time goes on, they will be able to identify bits of information in their environment through experience. You will notice that, as they get older, they can understand things a lot more than the previous year. So, patience is the key!

Child's Interests – Extracurricular Activities

Extracurricular activities can be seen as any activity done outside of school hours that does not include paid work, such as dance, singing, music, Boy Scouts, Girl Scouts, etc. It would be ideal to include this in your study programme because studying is more than just putting pen to paper or finger to keyboard.

You now have the freedom to expand your mind and explore the physical aspects. What might be right for your family may not be right for another family, but if as a family you enjoy trekking in the woods and being with nature, perhaps this could be included on a Sunday if you wish. Maybe every other Sunday if it's more convenient, you go out and learn about nature, the flowers, the bark of trees, the purification of air, etc.

This activity can be seen as a sport in itself as you are getting exercise and observing as you go along, it could be just what you need before you start the next week or to end a busy week. There is no point in creating a study programme that does not suit your lifestyle because chances are, it may be put to one side and forgotten. Remember, a study programme is a visual aid that allows you to put the learning into perspective so you can see what you would like completed on a daily basis for the week.

You make changes to it as your lifestyle may change or requirements for the day may change. You may have to rush around for the day, the child might have an appointment, then you have to do the shopping and as a result, not much learning is completed for that day. However, you may have done extra learning the day before or you will merge some of the learning into the following day if it's more suitable. You may also begin studying later than expected. I'm informing you of these variations in routine because this is normal and it will happen because life is full of surprises that take us off track, and that is okay.

Have an easy day as part of your weekly schedule. Including extracurricular activities into the schedule allows you to notice the variety of learning but also makes a day less challenging and the week more interesting. There are more after school clubs in different locations than ever before, such as ninja training, boxing, swimming, tennis, music, gymnastic clubs, etc. You can even have your child complete online zoom sessions on learning to play the guitar.

Everyone has become more resourceful and with a bit of research you can find little ways of incorporating third party learning into your lifestyle, and into your home. This also gives the child an opportunity to get out there and meet other children who are like minded, assuming they have the same interest in that activity. This is a great opportunity for the child to engage with others and challenge themselves with children of similar age.

Some of these activities may be expensive but there are more cost-effective ways through your local council. If you go online to your local council's website, they will have a section dedicated to families and children. You may be surprised what is available for your child on a weekly basis or even during school holidays, that are completely free. Get involved! Get active!

Culture Matters

The school environment doesn't explore enough about individual cultures. Religious education is focused on aspects of culture and religion; however, culture doesn't have to be religious, so there is a difference.

When you are homeschooling, you have the opportunity to explore other cultures as well as your own, for your child's benefit. Looking at your history and where you come from, can be part of the study programme. The library offers many resources on cultures around the world and may have a section dedicated to this topic. It's worth exploring and also using these books to read and compare with one another to get a greater an in depth understanding of the importance of culture and the history behind it.

The western world offers a very multicultural society where we are seeing many different cultures within one community and in some places up to 100 or more different languages being spoken. Each culture may be underpinned by principles and values, so understanding the distinction between them and the reasons why people live a particular way or have a particular view on life, can be interesting. While some cultures may be based on religion, others may not, and it can be helpful to recognise these distinctions when interacting with people in social or everyday settings.

As a result, your child will have that awareness and compassionate nature towards others. You may be even more tolerable to how some choose to live their life because knowledge is understanding. You do not have to agree with cultural aspects of people's lives but learning these aspects may enrich your lives and allow you and your child to engage with your community in a better way. Celebrating holidays are also included as a cultural experience.

Learning in depth about your own culture is very important. In my experience, I was able to go to the library and develop an in-depth knowledge through reading books to gain a better understanding of my history. I was then able to speak with my grandmother and she confirmed some things but also gave me her insight into our family history, which complemented the learning I had received.

An actual experience, that isn't always documented in books, can be very authentic because everything done in the past has come to shape our present. It's good to see how your cultural tradition has changed throughout the years but also how it started in order to document the change. As an activity, you could engage your child to compile a list of your culture's historical achievements. This will give your child a stronger foundation, and the ability to identify themselves as being part of something special, feeling more rooted in their heritage.

Time Spent

There is no specific time limit for how long you should spend on an activity or subject every day, or total number of specific hours for the week. Typically, a child is at school for 7 hours a day. A classroom might consist of 25 – 30 pupils. Imagine your child was the only pupil in a class at school. The tasks given would more than likely get completed sooner or your child could get through more tasks than usual. Therefore, most of the allotted study time at school would be insignificant. Perhaps a rough guide would be good if you are well structured and enjoy sticking to a time constraint or have other commitments that are at a set time on a weekly basis.

Alternatively, focusing on the activity or set work for the day without time constraints, allows your child to go at their own pace. Perhaps they can only complete a little at a time because they find the activity tough. That should also be considered because every child is different and the mind knows when it has had enough. Short breaks are key to being able to learn more. These breaks can be water breaks, play breaks or even nap time, depending on your child's age or ability.

You now have the opportunity to adjust the learning to your child's pace. School does give a good guideline as to where your child's learning ability should be, with the use of key stages, which you can use or refer to when needed. Your child can also then thrive if they are smart in a particular subject. For example, when I was 6 years old, I was encouraged to learn my timetables to 20 and achieved it effortlessly as maths was my strength, and so my ability was challenged because it was allowed in a private setting. There were no learning constraints and therefore, no guideline as to where I should be by a particular age. In turn, I did not encourage my child to learn his times tables to 20. He learnt them to 12 but found both 15x and 20x to be easy. He does not enjoy maths as a subject and so therefore, limits his ability to comprehend or explore it in my absence. However, yet again, the school's guidelines on timetables are up to 12x, so I know he is meeting the minimum.

I have created two study programmes for reference. Remember, going on visits to places such as museums is also time spent learning. Learning takes place all around us and you will find these opportunities naturally once you begin homeschooling. You may have a plan in mind of what to teach on any particular day, but in practice you may find your child is not particularly motivated on a specific morning every week.

This could be due to having English twice, next to each other. You may find your child does not remember problem solving skills in maths on Fridays, perhaps the last time you worked on maths was Tuesday or you only do maths once a week. You could then consider short bursts of maths throughout the week as an alternative. This way it's more constant but not too intense.

This is general guidance on how you may decide to make some changes to your study programme. A great idea is to end the week on revision, which encompasses what was learnt that week. As mentioned previously, revision is repetitive. Since it's not set in stone, it can always be tweaked and include the weekend, or perhaps a day off during the week. Looking back at something that your child struggled with during that week would be great review for the end of the week, with more sums or questions to help build a stronger foundation.

    *Remember, realistically, homeschooling requires less study time (up to 3 hours a day) because you are not in a school institution and have only your child or children to attend to. Learning opportunities are all around you. The rest of the day is yours to enjoy.

Child's Name

Home-School Planner 20....

Extra -Curricular 3:30PM
eLearning 4:30PM

Mon	Tue	Wed	Thu	Fri
English	I.T	Art	Science	Weekly Revision
English	I.T	Cultural Studies	Science	Weekly Revision
Math	Music	P.E	Extracurricular	eLearning
English	I.T	Art	Science	Weekly Revision
Math	Music	P.E	Extracurricular	eLearning
English	I.T	Cultural Studies	Science	Weekly Revision
Math	Music	P.E	Extracurricular	eLearning

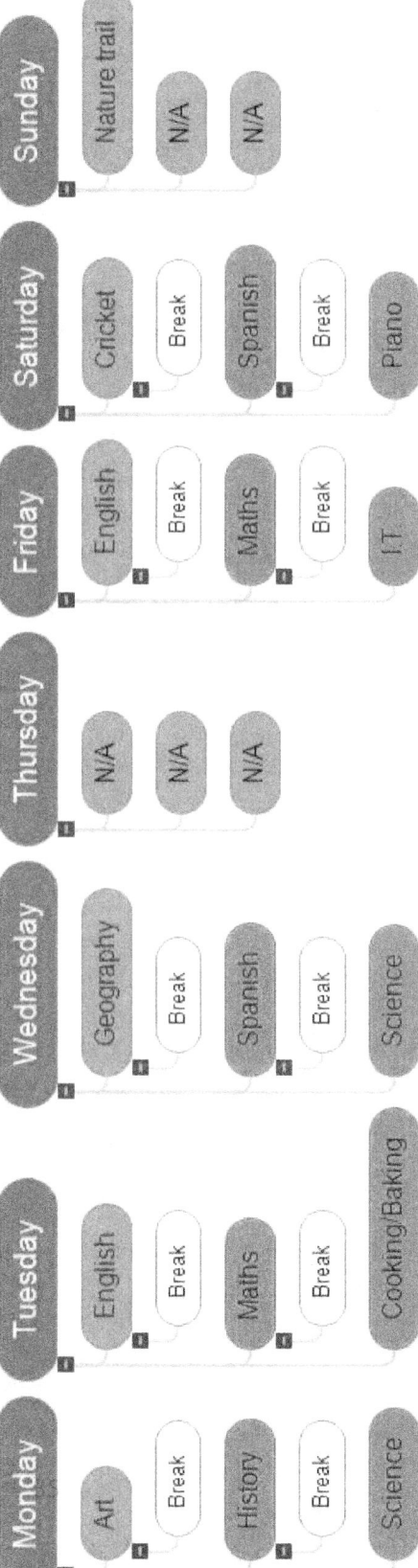

Maths English science art
History Geography Piano
Cricket I.T Spanish
Cooking/Baking

Homes-School Me
Study Programme 2

Monday
- Art
- Break
- History
- Break
- Science

Tuesday
- English
- Break
- Maths
- Break
- Cooking/Baking

Wednesday
- Geography
- Break
- Spanish
- Break
- Science

Thursday
- N/A
- N/A
- N/A

Friday
- English
- Break
- Maths
- Break
- I.T

Saturday
- Cricket
- Break
- Spanish
- Break
- Piano

Sunday
- Nature trail
- N/A
- N/A

Chapter 3

Is Homeschool Boring?

Yes and No! The creativity is with the parent, so if you have a mundane approach to homeschooling, then it can be boring for both you and your child. As seen in the previous chapter, I have presented two planners which offer very different methods for approaching homeschooling. It is best to tailor the planner to your child's interests and needs. Both are extremely important; your child's needs come first, which may contain core subjects or perhaps culture subjects, if that is compulsory for your child's needs. Needs are associated with what is essential for participation in society and will nurture the mind with knowledge and understanding in core subjects. For example, core subjects are seen as mathematics, English and science. They are essential for participating in society, as they are likely required to begin a college course.

Cultural studies can be a need rather than an interest if you would like your child to have knowledge and understanding of cultures in society, particularly in the western world where diverse cultures mix within boroughs, counties and communities. A need could be to emphasise your own culture, encouraging your child to understand who they are and where they came from. Cultural needs may include, how to live, eat and pray. These lifelong skills could help to define the character of the child, setting a strong cultural foundation. This can include, but is not limited to, a religious or spiritual foundation.

Interests matter because this adds to the value of enjoyment for the child as they are able to take it further with self-exploration. Also, interests on a particular day or day(s) gives something to look forward to. Interests can involve cooking, perhaps even specialising in continental dishes or cultural dishes. Maybe you've noticed your child take a keener interest in baking, why not try to bake different types of dishes; savoury or sweet.

Did your child enjoy baking bread? Why not try banana, choc-chip or pumpkin? This will be a great challenge for your child and gives them the opportunity to become an expert in what brings them joy. Interests are very important; just as important as needs. Whereas needs set the foundation, interests are what keeps us going in life. It's what we're willingly to choose to do with our lives in the end. Particular interests may include playing a sport or an instrument of choice. Choice is the key significance here because interests should be based upon free will. For example, if you decide your child should play the guitar but they prefer to learn to play the keyboard, then this is no longer an interest for them but for the you, the parent.

It is important to be mindful of these small decisions as they can be important to the nurturing process. As an adult we tend to explore our interests, so why not allow the same for our children. It is also important to note, that interests can develop skills in that area, which can be beneficial for competing, performing, or even self-fulfilment

How Do I Make It Fun

You don't have to be a great teacher to teach your child. What's great about a parent being a teacher is that no one knows your child better than you. Communication is key, so you already have the heads up on how best to communicate with your child because you do it on a daily basis. Pay attention to how your child reacts to different activities and most importantly their attention span. Every child is different and some may have learning difficulties which can involve neurological disorders, so it's important to be aware of your child's condition. Your recognition and dealing with any particular condition may be enhanced by doing some background research on how best to support your child, so you are equipped with the knowledge and understanding of your child's level of awareness.

Incorporate their learning with what they love and learn to share that interest with them. If, as a family, you prefer the outdoors, why not complete tasks in your garden or on your balcony if you have one. There are many science projects that explore the outdoors such as light and shadow science, where shadows are measured at different times of the day. If your child is obsessed with playing video games, perhaps research a good strategy game that allows them to use both their right and left side of their brain or even brain teaser games that force your child to think more.

This can help to improve their cognitive ability. There are also coding courses for children that help them learn how to create basic games and animation, such as "Scratch". This may be free within your community such as the library, or with your local borough/county. Alternatively, you can purchase the book and complete it as part of a walk-through with your child.

Social media has its problems and supervision is important but when used as an educational source, you can find the right connections to follow that hold valuable information for you and your child. This can help plant the seeds of success from an early age. Even TikTok has a wealth of information more incredible than school can offer, because sharing information digitally, is the new culture.

How Can Parents Enjoy Homeschooling

As mentioned previously, enjoying your child's interests with them adds to your enjoyment from homeschooling and helps to build a new bond with your child through learning. I find being prepared can make it easier, such as having your study programme in place. Therefore, the night before, you can see what you are focusing on for the next day. You can choose the required resources and have a clear outline on what part of that subject you are focusing on. It also gives you an opportunity to update your knowledge if needed, so you can better explain that topic or even look into different learning methods, especially in maths.

If you prefer the outdoors, travel and/or nature, you can incorporate it into your daily routine such as going to the park for play, exploring a forest, or even go on a field trip to a farm. These are just a few basic ideas of enjoyment but enjoyment can also be found inside the home i.e. board games. Most board games have an educational aspect such as Monopoly, The Game of Life, Scrabble etc. Making time for family fun activities should be part of your homeschool programme and can be weekly, fortnightly or even monthly.

Being part of a social homeschool group for parents can be positive. It is great for sharing ideas, meeting up and sharing moral support. Websites such as home-education.org.uk has resources for this purpose for the UK and nearby regions, including Europe. For the USA, you can visit the Homeschool World Forum.

Taking Breaks

Your child could get caught up in an activity, working hard towards answering questions or art work (which really helps to lose track of time). Taking a break helps you to recharge your energy (and interest), especially if it's a topic your little one is not fond of.

"Taking regular breaks like this allows us to stay energized throughout the day."
Shoukei Matsumoto, A Monk's Guide to a Clean House and Mind: Housekeeping Secrets from the World's Tidiest Monks

Breaks can involve water, rest, toilet, outside play, etc and best kept to anywhere from 10 minutes to 45 minutes. Too long and your child may not want to return to the activity; too short and it may not even feel like a break at all. This can be planned ahead of time. Let's say your child is completing a workbook activity and the target is to complete 4 pages.

Depending on the length of activity, you could then plan and decide that after two pages of work, it's time to take a break!

This can help to motivate the mind as it might feel overwhelmed if it is aware of a heavy schedule. Have you ever woken up in the morning and dreaded the day because you know it was going to be a busy day? I'm sure this happens time and time again for adults, whether it be work, or back-to-back meetings or even chores. Have you ever imagined how your child could be feeling knowing what is ahead of them for the day? Remember, your child is learning and you, the adult, has already learnt the information, so for somebody currently learning, their brain is trying to process all the information and make sense of it, jumping from activity to activity and subject to subject.

It is ideal for a parent to have good observation skills to observe their child's reaction to types of activities and workloads and see how they respond under pressure. Does your child have a short attention span? What activities or subjects do they enjoy the most? What types of questions take them longer to answer? When do they become frustrated? You may not have thought about these patterns of behaviour, but this book is designed to enlighten you so you can think about your child's overall wellbeing whilst being homeschooled. After all, you will be the only one observing them on a full-time basis and you want them to feel encouraged, not discouraged.

Spending Time Together

The opportunity to spend more time together through homeschooling is actually a great bonding experience. Tackling problem solving tasks and sharing opinions and views on literature does allow you to help shape your child's connection with the outside world.

Playing games is also important; there are many games that have an element of learning which includes strategy and logic. Articulate is a great way to stimulate your child's brain and won't even feel like learning because you will both be having so much fun. Also, if you remember any games from your childhood, it would be good to teach your child because you will remember how much fun you had and can share that experience. There's no limit to the fun. Its best to not be time restrictive, which is what makes it fun. The more the merrier! Include other family members and make dates for games and social activities.

Homeschooling is not about isolation. You may have other family members also homeschooling, and spending time with other parents and children enables the teaching process to be even more valuable. This can include visits to amazing sites around your home town, or even vacationing overseas. Yes, if money is not an issue you can homeschool anywhere in the world and you are not held to school holidays because a holiday is when it is appropriate for your family. The journey to another country is part of the experience, going through the airport and learning how the schedule works is quality time no matter the location. Cultural visits overseas, whether to your home country or to other peoples' is an experience your child will never forget. This can include excursions, sightseeing etc. Cherish the moment and opportunity with photographs or even create a scrapbook of fun times spent together.

Alternatively, touring your home town is equally fun and adventurous, from museums to obstacle courses, there are plenty things to do at home. Visit London (official visitor guide) also offers 101 best things to do with kids in London. There may be something similar where you reside, if you are living outside of London, or the U.K.

Having something to look forward to that's fun and adventurous for the month is very important because your child needs a challenge and an inviting schedule. From activities within the home to overseas activities, please do not feel pressured as a parent to compete with other parents, as your home and lifestyle is unique to you and you are doing the best that you can at the time. Children will understand if they cannot go camping or go to a beach in Spain.

Their true desire is for fun, and for them, that can be anywhere. Just try to remember yourself as a child and your fun memories. The first fun memory that comes to mind to me with my mother is her chasing us around the house, or playing monopoly. Quality time such as reading a book before bedtime is one of the most common daily routines a parent and a child could have, whether homeschooled or not. The simplest things in life can bring about the greatest pleasures!

Chapter 4

How Effective Can Homeschooling Be?

Homeschooling can be as effective as you make it. This means putting in the time to get the results. Your child may be struggling in a particular subject area i.e. English. As the teacher, you will be able to identify what areas of English your child is struggling with. Is it writing, spelling, or speaking and listening? As the teacher and observer, you can add extra sessions in your timetable to focus on problem areas. If you stick to your schedule, you cannot go wrong. Of course, schedules are not always easy to stick to, but being able to get back around to it is the key to seeing results.

Alternatively, you could hire extra support if English is not your first language, or you just struggle in this area. If you cannot afford the costs, look for free classes in your area via your local council and also on boards at your local shopping centre; they may be free or at a more affordable rate. It takes a village to raise a child, as mentioned before, please seek help from peers. Building your own study group can be beneficial in the long run as different people have different skill sets, So, collaboratively as a group of parents, you will be able to work effectively; even if its once a week or bi-weekly, every little helps.

Test Your Child

As you child progresses with the learning, it can be hard to tell how much information they are retaining along the way.

The word 'Test' may seem very school-like and formal but you could use a different term, such as, check or quiz. These are lighter choices of words so putting test in the same category can give it a less confrontational feel. This is because the word test can generate a feeling of nervousness, as it is something to be measured against. Not passing the test can make someone feel unworthy or not good enough. The idea of a test is to find out what information is being retained and understood.

Previously, when I helped prepare adult learners enrolling in basic English and math courses, I had to give them an assessment. This was essentially a test to see where their current level of understanding was in those subjects. Using the word assessment, as opposed to test, I believe made a significant difference to how people approached the situation. Test gives a warning that you have to have prepared for it. Often resulting in a pass or fail. Although the assessments given are essentially tests, as there is no pass or fail terms used when discussing results with learners, there were a number of questions to be answered correctly in order for the system to decide at what level of study to place the learner.

Had we used the term test, I believe we would have resulted in fewer learners completing the assessment, as many did not have prior knowledge. However, with the term assessment, learners were happy to complete the assessment at short notice without hesitation or fear of failing. We explained this was not a test they could fail, but an assessment that would help determine what level of study they need to begin at.

Terminology is very important, and so is delivery. You may think about these things when testing your child but I think it's good as a parent to allow them to feel at ease and apply positive connotations to testing and what it essentially means. If your child is taught that tests are nothing to be stressed about, this could be a good foundation for your child as they become older and have to take tests for different things such as driving tests, interviews, etc.

I was able to receive a yearly list of words that each year group at school should know how to spell. This was provided by a close family member whose son was of the same age and year group as mine. When she sent these words, I asked my son if he was familiar with them. Of course, he said yes. I decided to blindly test him on them, allowing him a sneak peek and then to repeat some key words back to me out loud.

Upon completing this task, I discovered that he was unfamiliar with some key vocabulary, and would misspell them on paper as well. I decided to break these words down into smaller groups, allow him to practice them, and then test him on them. I would give him a blank piece of paper, read out a word from the group we were working on and then give him a short time to write it down. As I read out the word, I am also repeating that word by placing it into a sentence as an example, so he can identify that word in his mind in a practical way.

Repeating this kind of activity has improved his spelling. He does not look forward to spelling but he is very good at it. This is an area I did not want him to struggle in, as I believe it is very important to be able to articulate yourself on paper. As a result, he is an amazing speller and enjoys the challenge. He is now comfortable pushing himself in this area.

Nevertheless, you can make testing fun. If your child enjoys spelling, then prepare weekly or bi-weekly spelling tests. Notice the words your child is misspelling or struggling with from time to time and jot them down on a piece of paper. After a while, you will have a collection of words and can also find similar words to add to this collection for a bigger challenge. Have your child study these words and when the time is right, test them on it and see how well they perform. This way of testing with spelling brings positive results because it focuses on words they tend to struggle with, so those words tend to not slip under the radar.

Successes In Homeschooling

Overall, both the UK and USA have seen homeschooling yield positive academic, social, and personal outcomes for many families. In the USA, many studies show that homeschooled students often out perform their peers on standardized tests. According to the National Home Education Research Institute, homeschooled students typically score 15 to 30 percentile points higher than the national average.

Homeschool is legal in all of the 50 states within the USA. According to 'myhomeschool' in the USA, Students homeschooling in the USA are the largest population of homeschool students globally. However, homeschooling is also on the rise in the United Kingdom Australia, New Zealand, India, Brazil, Canada, England, Japan, Mexico, South Africa, South Korea, Scotland, and Russia. Numbers have doubled in both the UK and Australia since Covid.

Research from the Office for National Statistics shows that homeschooled students in the UK often achieve higher GCSE results compared to their peers in traditional schools. Data reported by local authorities in the UK shows an increase in homeschooling, from around 56 000 in 2018 to 86 000 in the early months of 2024. The national Black Home Educators believes every child deserves a world class education and enjoy fellowshipping with parents, providing free resources and informs us on how MIT: Prestigious research university known for science, technology, and innovation, has free courses online from high school to graduate level, called 'Open Courseware'.

Wolsey Hall Oxford School is an online learning provider that claims to have assisted Nelson Mandela's studies for his London University law degree when jailed. Their prices may seem peak in comparison to other providers but their record appears outstanding and may be worth every penny. They are a registered online Cambridge International School that can take your child from age 5 through to higher learning with recognised qualifications worldwide.

iGCSE's/GCSE's can be taken as early as 12 years old, with the flexibility of homeschooling. A good idea in the UK is to choose 4 to focus on as this is the requirement for further education. Maths and English should be included as a choice. English and Science can both be taken as double or single award(s). Practice with past papers. There are some well-known names whose success can be attributed to homeschooling, such as:

- Abraham Lincoln (16th president of the United States)
- Serena Williams (One of the greatest professional tennis players of all time)

- Albert Einstein (theoretical physicist, awarded Nobel Prize in Physics)

- Leonardo Da Vinci (A famous painter, artworks include 'Mona Lisa' and 'The Last Supper')

- Alexander Graham Bell (inventor of the worlds' first telephone)

- C.S Lewis (The 'Chronicles of Narnia' writer)

- Taylor Swift (singer-songwriter celebrity and Grammy award winner)

There are plenty more, including those not as well-known but who have made significant successes in their lives, having been homeschooled. Your child does not have to become famous or receive really high grades to prove that homeschooling can be successful. A successful child is one that can be happy and educated to the extent of their ability. After homeschooling, a child matures into a young adult who explores options and forges their own pathways in life.

This is also true for individuals in institutions, but as a parent, you have the ability to construct and nourish their foundation, as a parent's love is the best love that a child can receive. This is one of the main reasons behind homeschooling, as parents want to be involved and ensure their child's overall wellbeing.

Chapter 5

Learning Approaches

Child-Led

When the learning is led by the child; this is a child-led approach to learning where the child's needs and wishes are taken into consideration when learning. This can make a really positive impact on learning for your child, as it creates a healthy and happy learning environment. To begin with this approach, you could create a chart or form, comprised of key questions for your child's individual learning plan. Otherwise known as an ILP, this can be tailored to your child documenting their likes, dislikes, needs, wants and wishes.

It's best to not limit your imagination when approaching this type of document because every child is unique and nothing should be seen as too odd or unnecessary. For example, if your child dislikes anything to do with mathematics in the morning, document this. If your child prefers English through online learning platforms, incorporate it. Vice versa. I hope you get the drift.

This approach will become more refined as you progress because you will learn your child's habits and then incorporate suitable learning methods to meet their needs. It would be ideal if they were also involved in putting the ILP together, which is part of the whole child-led approach. It's also about realistic expectations, so compromising with one another on certain inputs can also be good to ensure that you are still able to meet their needs and wants. The benefits of this type of approach can create a really happy and fun learning environment for the child, where the child thrives. Furthermore, you're able to see your child's capabilities in areas you would not otherwise have included. You may notice a skillset you can encourage, ensuring that you are not preventing your child from reaching their full potential. On the other hand, it could be challenging for the parent who may find some wants or wishes physically demanding, especially if the child prefers learning through play.

Parent-Led

When the learning is led by the parent, it is similar to the learning being led by the teacher, in school. Although the child's needs and wants are important, they are not the main focus because there may be a set of rules in place for which the child must abide by. These rules may focus on behaviour and attitudes to learning that do not fit every child but must be adhered to in order to meet the requirements set for learning.

For example, A parent-led approach may require two short 10-minute breaks and one 30-minute break for lunch.

Regardless of the child's wants in this case, the child will have to stick to the routine created by the parent as they are leading and decide what is best in this case. The pros to this approach are that the environment will be disciplined, and it has been proposed that such an environment can have a positive impact on a child's learning when the learning is monitored and structured. On the other hand, if a child's wants and wishes are not met, they could feel frustrated and possibly disengage with the learning. For example, my son uses mental maths as opposed to written maths. As long as he understands both, I'm okay with what he prefers.

Learning Styles

Having worked in education for over a decade, I've had to assess numerous students beforehand, so their specific learning styles are recorded. This normally takes place at the enrolment stage. Many people are unsure of how they learn best, even up to adulthood. Some people never take notice of this or even think about it. However, knowing your child's learning style and even knowledge of your own, is a good way to retain information. Most learning styles are part of a quiz, but as a parent, it is easy to find your child's learning style through observation.

There are three main basic learning styles; Auditory, Visual and Kinaesthetic. A fourth is known as Read/Write, part of the VARK model (1987) otherwise known as 'Verbal' but has not been commonly presented, in my experience. Your child may fit into one of these categories, or a combination of them. I have designed my own learning style questionnaire similar to those found online.

Learning Style Quiz

💬 Quick Tip: This quiz is for all ages but if a question does not apply, just skip it!

1.
When I am watching TV, I tend to:

A. Look at the characters and the background

B. Listen to watch the characters are saying

C. Prefer subtitles

D. Talk about it at the same time

2.
I can remember what to buy at the store with my pocket money by:

A. Seeing the images of what I want to buy in my head

B. Repeating what I want to buy in my head

C. Taking a written shopping list with me

D. Browsing shelves

3.
When I get a new device for the first time, I:

A. Look for a diagram or unboxing video online

B. Listen to the instructions out loud

C. Read the manual that came with it

D. Turn it on a figure it o

4.
I take better selfies when:

watch 'How to' videos

B. Discussing it with people I know

C. Reading top tips

D. I have several trial and error attempts until I find what works best for me

5.
If I want to be better at playing my games, I:

. Watch online videos of walkthroughs

B. Listen to other peoples advice

C. Read the instructions or research information online

D. Just get on and practice

6.
If I needed to find my way home, I would:

A. Look for familiar landmarks

B. Ask someone for directions

C. Read the road signs

D. Use a map

7.
I follow instructions better on how to make things when:

A. I watch a video or see images on how its done

B. I listen to someone telling me what to do

C. I read the instructions

D. I am involved putting it toget[her]

8.
I know I am doing well with my class work when:

A. I see my scores on a chart or table

B. My teacher/parent tells me I'm doing a good job

C. I read the written feedback on my work

D. I go throug[h] examples of completed w[ork]

9.
I find work easiest when:

A. Images and diagrams are included

B. The questions are read out loud to me

C. There's an explanation to read

D. We use equipmen[t]

10.
I prefer to be taught:

With pictures, diagrams and charts

B. By listening to my teacher or parent

C. By Writing notes, reading and completing workbooks

D. By doing activities, science experiments and touching things

11.
I can recall a book I have read before because:

A. I see the story in my head as pictures

B. I read it out aloud

C. I read the back of the books abstract

D. I discussed it with other people

12.
When I go to the dentist, I can better understand about my teeth if the dentist:

Shows me a diagram or images

B. Has a conversation with me where I can ask questions too

C. Gives me a leaflet to read

D. Uses a toy model to explain

For this learning style quiz, please keep your scores as to whether answers are mostly **As, Bs, Cs,** or **Ds**.

Please check your results below.

Mostly A ... Auditory

This is when the learner takes in information best through listening. They often exhibit strong listening skills, allowing them to retain and interpret information more effectively in auditory formats. This may include engaging with audiobooks, participating in conversations, and asking insightful questions to deepen their understanding. Additionally, I have tested learners with audio as part of speaking and listening exams, where I read a piece of information aloud. The learner is then tasked with recalling and summarizing what they remember from the listening exercise, providing valuable insight into their comprehension and retention abilities. Such methods highlight the importance of auditory learning in educational settings.

Mostly B ... Visual

This can occur on various platforms, whether it is a screen, printed paper, or any medium where the information is visually accessible. In addition to traditional texts, this learning style encompasses watching materials such as videos, plays, and using visual aids like pictures and posters. For instance, viewing a tutorial can be especially beneficial, as it allows learners to see each stage of a project clearly, while a handheld manual that combines images with text offers practical guidance. In classroom settings, this approach is often integrated into lessons through the use of engaging visuals on slides or short videos that enhance understanding of specific topics. Moreover, providing handouts, printed activities, books, and workbooks serves to reinforce learning by allowing students to engage with the material in a tangible way. This approach caters to diverse learning needs and promotes deeper comprehension.

Mostly C ... Verbal

This is when the learner takes in information by taking notes in class, capturing both what is said and what is visually displayed. They may also prefer to read a handout during lessons, as this allows them to underline or highlight key information, reinforcing their understanding. Furthermore, these learners often thrive in research projects that involve extensive reading, enabling them to delve deeper into topics of interest. The process of jotting down notes helps solidify their comprehension and retention of material, making it easier to review later. Additionally, incorporating structured activities, such as summarising or creating mind maps based on their notes, can further enhance their engagement and learning outcomes.

Mostly D ... Kinaesthetic

This is when learners take in information through active involvement, often referred to as being tactile. Such engagement can include hands-on activities like science experiments or participating in extracurricular classes that stimulate curiosity and enthusiasm. For core subjects like maths, this approach might involve practical applications, such as using real money or role-playing as a shopkeeper and customer to enhance money-calculating skills. Interactive play engages most of the senses, making it essential to get creative in meeting this learning need. For instance, visiting museums can provide valuable experiential learning opportunities, allowing children to explore various activities that reinforce concepts in a fun, memorable way. Additionally, incorporating outdoor activities, workshops, or community projects can further enrich their learning experience, fostering critical thinking and problem-solving skills. By blending creativity with hands-on learning, it can create an engaging environment that encourages exploration and deepens understanding.

Similar quizzes can be found online and should be done together with your child. These can be found in the resources section of the book. If you or your child fall into any one style, this does not mean that you cannot take in information any other way, it's just what suits your learning needs best. Using a variety of learning styles is always ideal when teaching as the pupil may learn a specific activity or topic better in a different style, or a combination of styles. For example, with my son, we looked at parts of a plant and their functions in a science textbook which was very visual as it had plenty images and diagrams. We also went to our local garden and explored the plants there, gently touching, smelling and making reference to the textbook, which was very kinaesthetic... It can be seen as an extension of the activity, so get creative!

e-Learning Or Workbooks

There is a range of e-learning software now widely available for children and adults. This is a more recent system of learning, incorporating the usage of technology. It's an alternative to workbooks; however, it can make use of work books but in a digital way. Many companies have created subject specific course content online for children to meet the national curriculum so they can learn as they grow. They can often include extras such as story books and printable worksheets.

One of the main advantages to e-learning is that it allows the user to go at their own pace and naturally adjust to their learning ability. Therefore, as their learning knowledge increases, the content becomes more advanced. This can be determined by how many questions you get right, timing, test results, etc. Each e-learning provider will offer unique processing tools. I have tried a range of e-learning platforms such as Reading Eggs, Explore Learning. Schools in the UK tend to use Rockstars, which focuses on timetables but with a rockstar theme to try to engage the children with the platform, using quizzes disguised as 'gigs' to make learning more fun.

Another advantage is having a live tutor via an online communication platform, like Zoom. Even parents who choose to send their child to school may seek an online tutor to support their child at home in areas they may be struggling with, such as mathematics. It's also useful to help your child to learn another language. What's even more valuable about that is the fact that the session can be one to one, so more attention is spent on your child's learning as an individual without any distractions. A website I've explored myself is *find tutors,* based in the U.K., where you can find a tutor for yourself or your child in a range of top subjects, including languages. For extracurricular activities like dance, skating, etc. I would advise you to also visit *super prof,* because it is well presented with tutors providing a self-presentation of their service, whether online or in person. Most importantly, their prices are transparent and some offer free or discounted first lessons. Children are used to being online today through coding, gaming and YouTube, so studying online shouldn't seem foreign to them.

Some of the disadvantages to consider with e-learning, which I've gained from firsthand experience, is connectivity issues. This can involve freezing, or not even being able to get onto a lesson as a result. You may be compensated for this but it can be an ongoing issue which can lead to frustration.

Workbooks

I strongly believe that successful schooling of any kind should involve workbooks or worksheets. Although, workbooks are more collectively organised. There are many brands of workbooks; some follow the national curriculum and some do not. Both are very useful when homeschooling, as they include a range of subjects. The advantages are, but not limited to:

- Improved handwriting capability
- Target practice questions

- Meeting the needs of visual and read/write learning styles
- Timed activities
- Can be seen as a learning guide
- For both active learning and easy revision
- No ongoing cost

Some well-known brands are the AQA, which is an awarding body for England, Wales and Northern Island. CGP provides workbooks for primary, secondary and A-level students. Collins offers an easy learning selection for parents to help their child learn at home for all ages and abilities. Workbooks tend to be accurate with answer pages towards the end of the book.

However, some workbooks do not fully explain the task at hand so it can be difficult for a parent to gauge how to complete the activity. For example, a workbook may ask the child to add prefixes or suffixes to a group of words listed below. However, if you have not yet discussed prefixes or suffixes, you will need to go elsewhere to explain this to your child beforehand. In my opinion, active learning should be included in the workbook to accompany this task before the activity is introduced, unless the workbook has a learning companion and it is the collaborative activity book.

Outdoors

The great outdoors is always full of adventure, especially for young minds. One thing for sure is that children look forward to playtime at school and it can be the highlight of their day. This can also be the same when homeschooling. If it's easier for you to get out early, then do so. There's no specific time because you construct your own timeline. However, your child needs to be able to run, climb, jump (if they can) because it strengthens their skills, and helps develop their awareness and physical ability. I have seen it firsthand. If your child is not interested in sports, then try martial arts or riding. Please find a list below of possible outdoor activity ideas:

- Skating (ice or no ice)

- Skateboarding

- Athletics

- Tennis

- Taekwondo

- Ninja Training

- Parkour

- Swimming

- Capoeira

- Basketball

- Football

- Netball

The Child's interests and personality should be considered. This should not be a forced activity because the aim is fun and not necessarily winning. If that is the focus then your child could excel and then focus on winning later down the line, but that also comes with its pros and cons. There is a class available for all the activities listed, and many more. You may have your child in a range of activities but be mindful of wearing them down. Children like to have fun, so trying out a range of activities or sports is a good idea, as a start to see what they naturally gravitate to.

Remember, if it's not fun for them, move on, it is not a competition! Try something different or similar if you are suspicious. Sometimes, it may be the teacher or environment they're not enjoying, and once that changes, you will see the change in them. It's good to be observant as a parent because these activities are typically not free so it's good to make sure your money is being well spent. Hopefully, your child can find an activity they enjoy!

Chapter 6

Learning To Read And Write

Reading

It's very possible to teach your child to read and write even if you've never been a teacher. If you possess these skills yourself, you can effectively pass them on to your children. Literacy is crucial in early childhood; the earlier it's introduced, the better the outcomes. When I began supporting adults in the community with basic literacy, starting from pre-entry level, I found that phonetics is always the best foundation. This refers to the sounds of letters, which is essential. Beginning with the alphabet provides a strong base.

Once your child can articulate the sounds of each letter, you can progress to blending sounds, focusing on simple two-letter combinations like T+H, which creates the 'Th' sound. There are many resources to assist in this journey. Flashcards from educational supply stores in the U.K., like 'The Works,' and in the U.S., such as 'Lakeshore,' can be very helpful. Additionally, musical CDs and online downloads focusing on phonetic language skills are widely available, along with Spotify playlists featuring popular children's characters like Gracie's Corner. These tools can make learning engaging and enjoyable for both you and your child.

With the flashcards and audio resources, you'll engage both visual and auditory learning styles, creating a comprehensive literacy experience. Your child will not only learn to recognize the shapes of the letters but will also start spotting them in their daily environment, reinforcing their learning. The audio materials, which resemble catchy nursery rhymes, make practice enjoyable and memorable. Children will likely recall the songs, which will help them remember the associated sounds. This method mirrors how I memorized my time tables as a child. As they read, your child may encounter challenging words that are difficult to pronounce. In such cases, encouraging them to write down these words on a separate piece of paper for further practice can be immensely beneficial. This strategy has proven encouraging for many students in the past, as it fosters a sense of accomplishment and boosts their confidence. By turning reading into an interactive and engaging process, you're setting a solid foundation for their lifelong learning journey.

Writing

You may be wondering why your child is able to read well but struggles with writing. This is actually quite normal, even among adult literacy learners. Many people who read proficiently still face challenges when it comes to writing or typing, even at the tertiary degree level. If your child is struggling with their handwriting, I would suggest practicing consistently. Repetition is key!

Setting aside a few minutes each day for focused writing practice can lead to significant improvement over time. Should my child learn cursive? As for whether your child should learn cursive, it really depends on their needs and interests. While some educators argue that cursive helps with fine motor skills and can aid in the development of a unique writing style, others believe that print is sufficient for everyday writing tasks and more suited for the new age. Ultimately, it's important to assess what will work best for your child and support them in a way that fosters their confidence and enthusiasm for writing.

We are increasingly moving away from handwriting skills and closer toward digital skills that prioritize typing and assistive systems, such as speech recognition software that can do the typing for us. While technology has its advantages, I believe it's still crucial to maintain the ability to hand write personal details, such as your name or a heartfelt note.

Handwriting is not just a skill; it's a form of self-expression that carries personal significance. My son, for example, struggled with cursive writing and ultimately shied away from it. He preferred writing his letters individually, which hindered the development of his handwriting skills and made his writing less legible for his age. However, this didn't impact his ability to produce grammatically correct sentences, as that is a separate area of learning.

I found that practicing cursive writing can greatly improve children's penmanship. It requires them to focus on the shapes of the letters and how they flow together on paper. Initially, they may write large letters, but with encouragement and constructive feedback, you can guide them toward writing smaller, more legible letters. Celebrating their progress and efforts fosters confidence, making the learning process more enjoyable. Overall, learning to write in both cursive and print allows children to develop their unique writing styles. This not only helps them recognize letters more effectively but also teaches them how different letters can be styled. By balancing both forms of writing, children gain a deeper understanding of language and develop a skill set that is valuable in both their personal and academic lives. Thus, nurturing handwriting skills should remain a priority alongside digital literacy.

Chapter 7

How To Keep My Child Motivated

Motivation Is The Key To Success

Motivation is the key to success. This well-known phrase resonates deeply in a homeschool environment, where it often falls on the parent to maintain high motivation levels. There will inevitably be days when you feel overwhelmed and lack the drive to engage fully with your child's learning, especially when other areas of your life demand attention. To ensure that the week runs smoothly, having a structured plan in place is essential. Once you've created your homeschool study programme (as discussed in Chapter 2), use the end of each week to review and outline the content for the upcoming week. This not only keeps you organised but also helps your child anticipate what's ahead, fostering a sense of security and readiness for learning. Think about Vygotsky's Zone of Proximal Development; is the work too easy or too difficult and how you can adjust it.

It's important to remember that the hours dedicated to homeschooling don't need to mirror those of a traditional school day. In fact, less time is often required, especially if you're homeschooling just one child. This allows for a more personalised and efficient learning experience, enabling you to focus on areas where your child may need extra help or enrichment. Moreover, incorporating breaks and varied activities can keep motivation high and make learning feel less like a chore and more like an adventure. Balancing educational goals with personal well-being is crucial; by doing so, you not only support your child's learning but also nurture your own motivation and enthusiasm as a parent. Sometimes it's a good idea to start the day with exercise, this is part of your weekly schedule and can include stretching, yoga, resistance, push ups or even weights depending on your child's age and fitness goals. This can help to wake up the body at the start of day and release tension and kickstart to a great day. This should not be long and strenuous and perhaps not every day but a good 15 – 20 minutes should be enough to feel energised.

Also, remember that learning is everywhere and does not always consist of sitting at a desk. Life skills are essential; for instance, involving your child in weekly shopping can be a valuable learning experience. Managing money, making decisions, and understanding budgeting all count towards their educational development. It's also important to include yourself as the parent in the homeschool environment, as you are not separate from the learning process. What motivates you each day? Perhaps it's music, playing an instrument, or enjoying a good novel

You can find creative ways for your child to learn by involving them in tasks you find pleasurable. Not only will this create bonding time, but it ensures that learning becomes an integrated part of your everyday life. For example, if you're a writer working on a novel, you could have your child sit beside you on their own laptop, introducing them to Microsoft Word if needed, and encouraging them to begin a short story of their own. You might set a challenge for them to write an opening paragraph while you focus on your own. This way, you achieve your goals while fostering a collaborative and supportive learning environment. Incorporating such activities not only enriches your child's education but also allows both of you to pursue your passions together, reinforcing the idea that learning can be both fun and meaningful.

Taking A Break

Breaking up the day with short breaks is an effective way to stay motivated and focused. The Pomodoro Timer has gained popularity in assistive technology and can be a valuable tool during homeschooling. This technique suggests 25 minutes of focused study followed by a five-minute break, making it easier for children to concentrate without feeling overwhelmed.

Research supports that short bursts of study are particularly effective in enhancing learning retention. However, if an activity is engaging and takes longer, you might consider extending the study period to 50 minutes, followed by a 10-minute break. Flexibility is key; what matters most is maintaining engagement and interest. I wouldn't recommend long study sessions without breaks, as children's attention spans are typically shorter than those of adults. This is especially true for children with learning difficulties, such as ADHD, who may require more frequent pauses to process information effectively. Incorporating movement or a change of scenery during breaks can also help re-energise them and prepare them for the next study session. By fostering a balanced approach to learning, you can create an environment that promotes both productivity and well-being.

Include playtime and activities (found in Chapter 5: Outdoors), as they help to break up the day and can transform it into a practical day filled with engaging hobbies. Many children today aspire to be gamers and may find themselves spending significant time playing games on PCs or consoles. Instead of viewing gaming solely as a distraction, you can incorporate it into their learning routine. Many modern games offer educational content that helps develop essential skills while keeping your child entertained.

For instance, some games on platforms like Roblox incorporate math skills, presenting users with questions that they must answer correctly in order to complete tasks and progress within the game. This creates an enjoyable learning experience that seamlessly integrates with their interests. To enhance this approach, consider researching the 10 best educational games for PC that align with your child's preferences. This way, you can provide screen time that is both enjoyable and enriching. Remember, the key is to ensure that the activities remain balanced and varied, fostering a well-rounded educational experience while also allowing your child to engage in the activities they love.

By blending learning with play, you not only keep them motivated but also enhance their overall development in a fun and interactive way. I would advise including longer breaks, such as half-term breaks, to help recharge both you and your child. These breaks can align with local school schedules or be customised to fit your family's lifestyle. If you choose to create your own breaks, this opens up opportunities for affordable holidays outside of peak times, when prices are typically lower. Not only does this make travel more affordable, but it also allows for enriching experiences away from the usual routine.

If you decide to stick to public school breaks, consider enrolling your child in local school holiday camps. These camps provide a fantastic way for your child to meet and play with other children, allowing them to develop social skills and form friendships outside of the home learning environment. In turn, this gives you, as a parent, a well-deserved break to recharge and focus on your own needs. Ultimately, through trial and error, you will discover what works best for your family's unique situation and lifestyle, ensuring a balanced approach to education and personal well-being. Finding that equilibrium is crucial for maintaining enthusiasm and motivation in both you and your child.

Chapter 8

How Do I Balance The Time?

Study Materials

Your main learning activities are most likely a mixture consisting of:

- Workbooks

- Quizzes

- e-learning

With homeschooling, you'll find it quicker to get through a subject or activity compared to traditional schooling. For example, a teacher may set a task for children to complete that takes 45 minutes as a class; however, that same task may take you and your child just 20 minutes. This is because the focus is on one child or a small group rather than an entire classroom. This doesn't imply that it's best to pack as many activities as possible into the day. In fact, there should always be time for breaks and opportunities for free play in your daily schedule. This approach gives both you and your child a chance to relax, recharge, and engage in unstructured learning, which is just as important for their development.

Additionally, it's beneficial to incorporate hands-on activities or nature walks to enhance learning and foster curiosity. Handy homeschool planners can be found in Chapter 2 to assist you with a structure that may be useful if you haven't got the foggiest idea where to start. Please use these planners and be creative with them to fit your lifestyle, ensuring that each day is not only productive but also enjoyable and enriching for both you and your child.

A typical day at homeschool should begin with breakfast. I'm including this in the schedule because it's very important not to skip breakfast just because you're at home, regardless of whether your child feels hungry or not. If they aren't particularly hungry, consider offering something very light, such as yoghurt or fruit, or waiting some time before having a proper breakfast and starting the day's studies.

My son is a late eater and generally doesn't have much of an appetite in the morning. I can relate to this, as I was the same as a child; my mum often had to encourage me to drink tea before I left the house. When I've allowed my son to skip breakfast, I've noticed a sudden decline in his energy shortly after beginning work. He then requests something to eat, which interrupts his focus and flow. Therefore, it would be ideal to start studies after breakfast, even if breakfast happens closer to brunch time.

This can change as they get older. They still may not have a morning appetite but can manage work better on an empty stomach. However, if you don't have time for a full meal, a cup of tea or some orange juice can provide a reasonable amount of energy to kick start the day. Then, perhaps schedule in a short

30-minute break for a snack. As every child is unique, you have the flexibility to tailor this routine to fit their needs. To ease them into the day, consider starting with a light activity, such as reading a book or watching a documentary, which can stimulate their minds before enjoying something to eat. This gentle start can create a more engaging and productive homeschooling environment.

After breakfast or brunch, your schedule may include English, a break, maths, lunch, and an outdoor activity like going to the park. I've found that after engaging in outdoor play, children often have reduced energy levels, making a light activity such as reading a chapter of a book a more manageable option. This allows them to wind down without feeling overwhelmed. Following the reading and discussing the chapter is an excellent way to assess their understanding and encourage critical thinking.

For older children, such as teens, it's important to adapt activities to suit their age and interests, ensuring they remain engaged and motivated. The time it takes for your child to complete these activities will vary significantly based on their individual learning style and pace, and it's likely to differ from the time you initially set aside. You may not be able to complete workbooks and e-learning on the same day, so it might be more effective to designate specific days for e-learning.

E-learning typically involves a considerable amount of screen time, and the blue light emitted from computers can lead to eye strain, commonly referred to as computer vision syndrome. To mitigate this issue, I strongly recommend using a blue light filter, which can help ease any strain on the eyes. Controlled timing when using a PC is also advisable; consider implementing regular breaks to allow for rest. Many computers have built-in filters available under the Night Light setting, which can automatically adjust the screen's light emission based on the time of day. This thoughtful approach not only enhances comfort but also promotes a more sustainable and enjoyable learning environment for your child.

Being Creative

As discussed in the first chapter, learning is all around us. This presents a wonderful opportunity to be creative and incorporate educational experiences into various trips and occasions. Let's say you are embarking on a long family road trip. There are countless opportunities to teach your child valuable skills, such as tallying. For example, you can have them tally the different types of vehicles that pass by or focus on counting vehicles of various colours. If your child is older and able to sit in the front seat, you can engage them by pointing out landmarks and road signs that guide your journey. This can help them develop a sense of direction and geography.

Encourage them to set up the satnav or use an A-Z road atlas. It's essential to have a backup map book, as technology can sometimes fail; just make sure it's the latest edition, since roads frequently change and maps can become outdated. Additionally, explaining the rules of the Highway Code, including how different lanes function, can be an invaluable lesson. This not only prepares them for future driving but also instils a foundational understanding of safe driving practices. By observing the road and discussing what you see, you can spark their curiosity about driving and instil a sense of responsibility. This interactive approach transforms a simple car ride into a rich learning experience, laying the groundwork for their future adventures on the road.

Things that tend to take more time are videos, hands-on activities such as painting, drawing, and cooking. These engaging methods not only deepen understanding but also foster creativity and practical skills. Additionally, going outside for outdoor activities can provide a refreshing change of pace and enhance overall well-being. Schedule in time to reflect on what has been achieved over a course of time. Acknowledging both big and small accomplishments can motivate both you and your child to continue learning. This reflection is an important part of the learning process. Perhaps a reward for progress could include a fun day out, allowing you to celebrate achievements together while creating lasting memories. Incorporating these elements into your homeschooling routine can make the experience more enjoyable and fulfilling for everyone involved.

Chapter 9

How Do I Know If My Child Is Learning?

As a tutor, evidence of learning is usually documented and can take the form of observations, assignments, workbooks, and other materials. When homeschooling, any evidence of learning serves not only to benefit your child but also to help you in your reviews of their progress. Although homeschooling tends to be more flexible, with fewer regulations and oversight compared to traditional education, it's still beneficial to keep records. Practicing this documentation can provide structure and help you track your child's development effectively.

Creating a logbook for report writing can be an excellent way to organise your observations and insights, while maintaining a folder of previous work allows you to showcase their accomplishments over time. This system can also make it easier to reflect on areas where your child excels, or may need additional support. Furthermore, having a record of progress can be motivating for your child, as they can visually see how far they have come. Ultimately, establishing a routine for documentation will not only enhance the homeschooling experience but also empower both you and your child as active participants in their educational journey.

Logbook

A logbook could simply be an A4-style diary, but a more effective version would be an A4 project notebook designed for home, office, and school use. This type of notebook often features coloured tabs that separate sections, making it easier to organise your notes by subject. This method can enhance clarity and accessibility, allowing you to quickly find relevant information when needed. It's entirely your choice how frequently to log performance - daily, weekly, monthly, or bi-monthly - so long as each entry is dated to track progress over time effectively. Alternatively, you could create an A4 chart in Word, taking into account your child's strengths and weaknesses. This visual representation can help you set clear, achievable goals and monitor development. Ensure that your projections are reasonable and tailored to your child's abilities, keeping in mind their learning style and pace.

Flexible timescales are essential; they prevent unnecessary pressure on both you and your child, maintaining the focus on learning rather than stress. Ultimately, this documentation not only serves as a valuable record of progress but also fosters a supportive learning environment where growth and improvement can flourish without feeling overwhelming.

Folder

A folder can showcase your child's achievements over time, serving as a tangible reminder of their hard work and progress. It's incredibly encouraging for both you and your child when completed work is placed inside, as looking back through the folder reveals clear evidence of growth. This collection can include a mixture of artwork, English assignments, and maths exercises, although you may prefer to keep subjects separate for better organisation. This structure allows you to observe the diverse skills your child has developed alongside the range of topics you've covered together.

Moreover, I find it useful to use the folder as an opportunity to prepare a yearly test on what has been learned and understood. This not only refreshes your child's memory but also enables them to revisit chapters or concepts they may have forgotten, helping them to brush up on their skills. To stay organised, consider jotting down a date in the calendar as a reminder for the review. Additionally, purchasing a test book with questions and answers tailored to the curriculum can be highly beneficial. Completing these exercises within a set timeframe can serve as effective revision, reinforcing what your child has learned. Engaging with this material actively can boost their confidence, making learning more enjoyable and meaningful. By incorporating these strategies, you create a comprehensive learning experience that supports your child's ongoing development and fosters a love for learning.

Chapter 10

Practice And Repeat

It's typical for your child to forget what was previously studied. Having completed many workbooks throughout the years, I've noticed the repeat pattern as the level/age increases. The topics are the same but may require more from your child. Nevertheless, there is a clear repetition of information. This requires memory recall, which in my opinion, is how the school education system works. When I was preparing for my GCSE's, I decided to revise and summarise each class into notes. I then stuck my notes onto different sections of the walls in my bedroom; each representing the different classes.

For revision, I simply read my summarised notes the day before my exam in the morning. This was easy as all the background work was completed ahead of time such as the sorting and organising of my revision. As a visual learner, I could create a picture-perfect image of what was on my wall at home and put the correct notes into my exam. As a result, I passed all my GCSE exams with A-C grades, which were pass rates at the time. This method is useful at secondary school age and can be useful at primary school age if you are testing your child on what they have learnt for the year to prepare and become used to summarising and organising notes.

Handwriting Skills

Should you be concerned about your child's handwriting skills? With the increase in technology, some schools prepare work on devices such as tablets, PC's, etc. When homeschooling, you may use a mixture of devices but more simply, you are likely to teach your child the traditional way, using pen to paper, because it's easier to get your learning points across this way. Especially with maths, which could have you explaining different ways to calculate a sum as part of working out. This also includes the use of a whiteboard. They can come in small sizes as well as large sizes. Nevertheless, your child may need to improve on their handwriting skills. Their motor skills play a big part in the handwriting area including cursive writing.

With more use of technology in school and also at home, it's easy to become less focused on handwriting skills. This is because they are handwriting less and perhaps typing more, due to the increase of technology in education. My son is a passionate gamer who enjoys using the PC for long stretches, often preferring to stay glued to the screen if given the chance. While he excels in the English language, he has a strong aversion to writing, viewing it as a chore rather than a valuable skill. I never had the neatest handwriting myself and still struggle with it today. However, I firmly believe in the importance of practice and improvement, and I encourage my son to enhance his writing skills. I see this as one of his weaknesses, a common issue parents might notice with their own children.

In today's digital age, children tend to write less and type more. Texting, in particular, has transformed our language; acronyms and short hand dominate conversations because they are quicker and easier. While this has its conveniences, it can also lead to a decline in handwriting skills. The art of penmanship can easily become neglected, resulting in handwriting that becomes increasingly illegible over time, especially when not practiced regularly.

To address this, I try to incorporate fun and engaging activities that inspire him to write more, such as having him develop game reviews or storylines. He wrote his own short story book based on his interests, and included artwork. I believe this activity encouraged him to write more. At a young age, they can have quite an imagination so they are able to flow pretty well. By making writing a more enjoyable part of their daily routine, you can help them to foster a sense of pride in their work and help them develop a skill that will serve them well in the future.

Handwriting may seem less relevant in a tech-driven world, but it remains a fundamental skill that can enhance communication and creativity. Scheduling handwriting opportunities is essential to improving handwriting skills. Workbooks are helpful because they allow practice and repetition when answering questions. Handwriting books are more useful in early stages of development rather than after, as they work on the child's motor skills with repetitious patterns. As the child gets older and their motor skills improve, the practice of writing sentences is where you will be able to spot the inconsistencies.

I utilise homeschooling as an opportunity to incorporate cursive writing into our daily routine. My son despises this type of writing and feels that individual letters are much easier, but I took the time to show him how much faster cursive writing can be in comparison. Although it's not his preferred style, I firmly believe in the numerous benefits it provides. Research suggests that the process of writing in cursive can help reinforce memory and understanding, both of which are critical for learning. I've noticed that writing in cursive increases his active engagement in English comprehension significantly. There's an undeniable focus on the material he's writing, and I also highlight to him his growth in fine motor skills.

Fine motor skills can take time to develop for some children, while others may thrive at an early age. Some, like myself, may never fully master the best techniques, but I can confidently say that I possess the skills and understanding to write in cursive and read various signature styles. This knowledge not only benefits my writing but enriches my appreciation for different forms of handwriting. Continuing to practice cursive can instil a sense of resilience, showing them that perseverance can lead to mastery, even in areas that initially seem challenging or unappealing.

Chapter 11

What Type Of Support Is Available?

Homeschooling opens the door to innovative thinking, allowing parents to step beyond conventional educational boundaries. This unique approach can spark creativity and encourage you to explore diverse learning methods, deeply engaging with your community along the way. Traveling with your child amplifies this experience, as you encounter families who share your perspective, fostering inspiring conversations about different lifestyles and educational choices. Each journey not only builds confidence in your homeschooling decision but also highlights the vastness of the world compared to the rigidity of traditional school routines. Through these shared experiences, your child learns that education is not confined to textbooks; it's woven into the fabric of everyday life, enriching their understanding of the world.

As the primary supporter in your child's educational journey, you play a pivotal role in nurturing their independence. Homeschooling eliminates the daily commute, providing more opportunities for practical learning, like navigating local areas or using public transport. Since school is at home, they won't need to commute to school every day like other children their age so it is important to recognise that supporting them with their travels is part of the homeschool journey.

Teaching them essential skills like crossing streets and finding their way becomes a shared adventure that instils confidence and fosters problem-solving abilities. You can involve them in planning outings, discussing safety measures, and mapping routes, turning every trip into a valuable lesson. While it may feel daunting to send your child out alone, especially if you have only one, this gradual process is crucial for their growth and self-discovery. As they practice these skills, you'll notice their confidence blossoming. Utilizing tools like GPS can ease your concerns, empowering them to explore and develop self-reliance in a safe, structured way. Each small step they take toward independence is a victory worth celebrating.

This journey not only helps them build essential life skills but also strengthens the bond between you, as you navigate challenges together. Embrace the journey, allowing your child to learn from their experiences and mistakes, and watch them flourish into confident, capable individuals ready to embrace the world around them! The homeschooling experience is not just about academics; it's about fostering resilience, creativity, and a lifelong love of learning.

Community

- Check with your local council or state for free tuition in maths and English. These valuable sessions are likely to be available in the evening, as most children are at school during the day. As part of the government's commitment to education, they should provide free projects for the community or for a nominal fee, making it easier for families to access important learning resources without a significant financial burden.

- Flexi-schooling is a unique blend of part-time school and part-time homeschool. While children may still need to attend five days a week, they typically do so for shorter hours each day compared to those in full-time school. Whatever the arrangement, it can be especially beneficial for families who find it challenging to balance work commitments and homeschooling simultaneously. With flexi-schooling, you can enjoy greater control over the schedule, allowing for more personalized learning experiences. Any parental input can be significant, as your involvement can enhance your child's education and foster a stronger connection between home and school.

- In the UK, if your child is aged 14 or older, some colleges allow your child to attend, to focus on a specific subject. In The USA, this is called 'dual enrolment program' where the child can earn college credits and reduce costs. This can also be free in some cases. (Please see chapter 13: Useful Resources).

- Visit your local library and see what short courses are available. These are sometimes offered in person or online, providing a flexible learning option. Either way, it should be completely free and can easily fit into your weekly schedule. Courses may run for several weeks at a time, but they're usually not advertised well. It's best to pop in and speak to a friendly member of staff, who can guide you through the offerings, and browse their bulletin boards to discover what's available that you could sign your child up for. Engaging in these courses can enrich your child's learning experience and expose them to new interests.

- Check community boards in your area, such as those within your local shopping centre, as they often provide advertising opportunities for free. These boards are designed for the community to engage with one another and may feature valuable resources or events for your child nearby. You might discover lessons in languages, musical instruments, or even sports activities, often available for a fraction of the price compared to online options. By keeping an eye on these boards, you can find enriching opportunities that may not be widely advertised, allowing your child to explore new interests and develop skills in a supportive local environment. Engaging in community activities can also foster friendships and connections with peers.

- Utilise your friends and family as valuable resources in your child's education. Perhaps they know a trade or skill that could benefit your child. They may play an instrument, excel in cooking, or have good practical skills in the home, or on the PC. If you ask, you shall receive! Many might be willing to offer some of their time to share their knowledge with your child or even take your child or children out for the day as part of practical learning experiences. Hands-on learning is always ideal for getting children motivated and engaged. Days out can include various tourist activities, such as visiting cultural landmarks or attending local events. This is a wonderful opportunity to immerse your child in the rich culture of your community, exploring famous buildings, museums, and the unique adventures the city has to offer. Such experiences can ignite a passion for learning and create lasting memories.

e-Learning

- Superprof.com and findtutors.co.uk is the UK version to finding a lesson in almost any subject. This can be both face to face or online. All ages are welcome. Some first lessons can be free. Costs are usually charged by the hour but would be a one-to-one lesson for your child in almost anything of interest. This is also a good option if you would like your child to brush up on skills they already have e.g. basketball. Perhaps a one-to-one session will help your child gain valuable skills and techniques to boost their confidence in the current team they play for. What's good about these lessons is that if you have more than one child or your child has a friend, they can join in too.

- Takelessons.com is available in the USA to find tutors for almost anything. It includes both practical and non-practical learning opportunities, from musical instruments, languages, and academic subjects. These lessons can be private, grouped, or videos.

- Udemy offers a wide range of online courses for a small fee, making learning accessible to everyone. These courses vary greatly and are categorized into different skill levels, ensuring there's something suitable for everyone. This platform presents a valuable opportunity to gain new skills from instructors worldwide, benefiting both adults and children alike. Among the many offerings, there are several popular Roblox courses tailored for kids interested in coding or building games on the Roblox platform. These courses can spark creativity and provide practical knowledge, helping children develop valuable skills that can be useful in future careers in technology and gaming.

- Visit alison.com for free courses online, some of which can be useful for your child such as Microsoft Office, etc.

Some courses are accredited but all offer certification at a small fee.

Resources

- There are many documentaries available online, such as those from National Geographic Kids, YouTube, or even in your home if you have Netflix. Explore documentaries that are both useful and child-friendly, catering to various interests and age levels. Ask your child what type of documentary intrigues them the most. This is a wonderful way to observe and understand the world around them. After watching, you can create engaging activities or thought-provoking questions related to the program. Most importantly, take the time to discuss aspects of the documentary together, which can help identify any evidence of learning and deepen their understanding of the subject matter. Engaging in these discussions fosters critical thinking and encourages a lifelong love of learning.

- Scour the internet for "Free Homeschool resources." This can be done through a simple Google search or by checking the useful resource section in Chapter 13. You could even search online under images for printable worksheets that align with various subjects. Additionally, there are several websites that offer a yearly fee for access to a wide range of resources. A fantastic free option is from Learning Resources UK, which also has a US site link, providing valuable tools for both regions in different subjects such as STEM, English, maths, and coding. Exploring these resources can help you create a diverse and engaging curriculum tailored to your child's learning style and interests, enhancing their educational experience.

Chapter 12

Things To Remember!

Here is a list of key things to remember when homeschooling, which have been mentioned throughout the book.

The Importance Of Water

Water breaks or simply having a drink of water on the desk within reach is incredibly helpful for maintaining focus during lessons. Brain MD explains that since your brain is primarily composed of water, staying hydrated can significantly enhance concentration, boost cognitive function, and reduce stress levels. Proper hydration also supports overall health, contributing to better mood regulation and improved energy levels throughout the day. For even more insights, you can explore Brain MD's resources to discover additional reasons for the myriad benefits of drinking enough water regularly. Making hydration a priority can be a simple yet effective strategy to optimize your child's learning environment.

Breaks

Take as many breaks as needed throughout your homeschooling day. The Pomodoro technique suggests studying for 25 minutes followed by a five-minute break, but feel free to adjust this to suit your child's unique needs. This method aims to boost concentration and can help maintain focus during lessons. Regular breaks not only refresh the mind but also provide opportunities for movement, which can further enhance cognitive function and learning retention.

Observe Behaviour

Pay close attention to your child's behaviour. Are they getting hungry, tired, or even a bit miserable? These are clear signs that it's time for a break or to stop altogether. It's essential to go at your child's pace and create an environment that encourages learning without pressure. Remember, you're not competing with the standards of traditional school education, as homeschooling offers a different approach tailored to your child's strengths and interests. Focusing on a small, manageable skill set can often be more effective and memorable than trying to cover a wide range of topics that may lead to confusion or overwhelm. Emphasising depth over breadth allows your child to master concepts and skills at their own rhythm, ultimately fostering a love for learning and a sense of accomplishment. Encouraging this personalised learning experience can lead to greater confidence and motivation in your child's educational journey. Regardless of a parent-led or child-led approach, teaching your child obedience with their work will help them in the future.

Allow Changes To The Schedule

Don't be too rigid with your homeschooling schedule. While it's great to have educational targets, don't be afraid to manipulate or adjust your plans as needed. This flexibility is a key part of the freedom that homeschooling offers! Life can be unpredictable, and some days may call for a different focus or a break from the norm to keep things fresh and enjoyable.

Must Include Child's Interests

A schedule that lacks interest can make it incredibly difficult for your child to retain information. For example, if your child does not enjoy maths, consider not spending all day on it. Instead, find creative ways to engage with your child's preferred learning style, making the subject matter more enjoyable and relatable. Incorporate activities or subjects they find exciting; perhaps your child has developed a keen interest in robotics. While you may have little knowledge in this area, there are many resources available online, in bookstores, and in local libraries to support this interest. Encourage your child to spend time researching robotics, allowing them to take the lead in their learning journey. They are never too young to dive into a passion!

Think about shows like Junior MasterChef, where young chefs across the country compete to impress judges with their culinary creations. These examples highlight how kids can explore and develop their interests in meaningful ways, nurturing their talents and fostering a love for learning. By allowing your child to follow their passions, you create a more dynamic and engaging educational experience that not only enhances their knowledge but also builds confidence and independence.

Revision, Revision, Revision!

This is the key to success for exams and tests. Going back over things already covered is not going backwards; it's looking back in order to move forward. Revisiting previously learned material reinforces knowledge, solidifies understanding, and builds confidence in your child's abilities. Please take the information in this book as key advice and a blueprint for effective homeschooling. If you decide to homeschool into secondary school and/or high school, remember that many families have successfully navigated this path before. If you find the schooling system becoming increasingly strict with age, and it's not resonating well with you or your child, it's important to recognise that it's never too late to return to homeschooling.

This transition could be a significant step in the right direction for your family, offering a more tailored and supportive learning environment. Embracing homeschooling at any educational stage allows you to create a learning atmosphere that prioritises your child's unique needs, interests, and pace. By doing so, you not only cultivate a love for learning but also empower your child to thrive academically and personally, ultimately setting them up for success in their future endeavours.

Chapter 13

Useful Resources

101 things to do with kids in London - visitlondon.com

https://www.visitlondon.com/things-to-do/family-activities/101-things-to-do-with-kids

Alison Free Online Courses

https://www.alison.com/

Autodidact Definition & Meaning - Merriam-Webster

(https://www.merriam-webster.com/dictionary/autodidact)

Collins Easy Learning Workbooks Collection
(https://collins.co.uk/collections/collins-easy-learning-workbooks)

Colour My Learning
https://www.colourmylearning.com/2020/07/15-successful-people-you-didnt-know-were-homeschooled/

Education Act 1996
https://www.legislation.gov.uk/
https://www.legislation.gov.uk/ukpga/1996/56/contents)

Education Otherwise - Education is Compulsory School is Optional
https://www.educationotherwise.org

Elective Home Education Statistics UK
https://explore-education-statistics.service.gov.uk/find-statistics/elective-home-education

Home Education – child law advice
https://childlawadvice.org.uk/information-pages/home-education/

Home Education UK: Forums
https://www.home-education.org.uk/ (https://www.home-education.org.uk/forums.htm

Homeschooling in the USA

https://myhomeschool.com/us/

Homeschool World Forum - Index page

https://www.homeschool.com/

(https://www.Homeschool.com/forums/

How to Earn College Credit Through Dual Enrollment

https://www.usnews.com/education/articles/how-to-earn-college-credit-through-dual-enrollment)

Illustrated GCSE revision guides

https://clearrevise.com/

Kids National Geographic

https://kids.nationalgeographic.com/

Lakeshore Teacher Supply Store | Top-Quality Learning Products

https://www.lakeshorelearning.com/

Learning Resources UK & US

https://www.learningresources.co.uk/free-activity-sheets-for-kids

https://www.learningresources.com/

Learning Style Tests for Children

https://kids.lovetoknow.com/wiki/Learning_Style_Tests_for _Children

Learning Styles Quiz: What Is Your Child's Learning Style? – Teacher Lists Parent Corner

https://www.teacherlists.com/blog/parent-corner/what-is-your-childs-learning-style-quiz

Maths Worksheets KS3 & KS4 Printable PDF Worksheets

https://www.cazoommaths.com/

(https://www.cazoommaths.com/maths-worksheets/)

National Black Home Educators

https://www.nbhe.net/

Oxford Home Schooling UK Provider of KS3, GCSE, & A Level Courses https://www.oxfordhomeschooling.co.uk/

Private lessons and tutors

https://www.findtutors.co.uk/

Practice with past papers, English, Maths and Science

https://mmerevise.co.uk/

Psychometric Tests – Open Psychometric Test Resource

https://www.openpsychometrics.org/

Research Facts on Homeschooling – National Home Education Research Institute https://www.nheri.org/research-facts-on-homeschooling/

Superprof - Find Private Tutors & Personal Tutors for Home Tuition https://www.superprof.co.uk/

Take Lessons
https://www.takelessons.com/

The King's Speech 2024 - GOV.UK
www.gov.uk https://www.gov.uk/government/speeches/the-kings-speech-2024

The Works Get Huge Savings On Arts, Crafts And Books
https://www.theworks.co.uk/

Twinkl – Primary and secondary resources free and paid
https://www.twinkl.co.uk/

VARK Learning Style Questionnaire: How do you learn best?
https://vark-learn.com/the-vark-questionnaire/

Udemy
https://www.udemy.com/

Wolsey Hall Oxford: The Homeschooling College

https://wolseyhalloxford.org.uk/

Worksheets for practicing handwriting

https://www.worksheetworks.com/

CONTACT THE AUTHOR

If you have enjoyed the book, want to leave feedback, comments or have any questions, please get in touch via email at fresh817@aol.com. I look forward to hearing from you.

I hope this book has helped answer some questions you may have had, as well as some useful tips going forward to prepare you on your homeschool journey. Don't be afraid to make mistakes! I wish all readers the best possible outcome.

Printed in Great Britain
by Amazon

62677914R00085